Cesar Chavez

Mark Falstein

GLOBE FEARON

Pearson Learning Group

Freedom Fighters

Cesar Chavez
Fannie Lou Hamer
Martin Luther King, Jr.
Malcolm X
Nelson Mandela

Editor: Tony Napoli
Production editor: Joe C. Shines
Cover and text design: London Road Design
Production: ExecuStaff

Photographs: Cover—UPI/Bettmann Newsphotos; pp. 12, 44, 65—The Bettmann
Archive; pp. 47, 56, 68, 72—AP/Wide World Photos

ISBN 0-8224-3223-4
Printed in the United States of America
7 8 9 10   05 04 03 02

Globe
Fearon

Pearson Learning Group

Contents

CHAPTER 1
Migrants

They were always moving. They followed the seasons and the crops. Spring for the Chavez family began in the lettuce fields of California's Imperial Valley. Then they traveled north and west, picking vegetables in the Coachella and San Bernardino valleys. Summer found them in the vineyards of the great Central Valley, following the ripening grapes north. In the fall they came south again, to the orchards and tomato fields near Oxnard.

They lived in labor camps. Sometimes they were lucky enough to find one with showers and clean beds. But the work in such places seemed never to last long. Soon they were on the road again, moving on to the next job. They slept in their car. It was an old Studebaker that kept breaking down. Sometimes they slept in tents or under bridges. The life of a migrant farm worker did not give a person a sense of home or community. It did not encourage book learning either.

By the time Cesar Chavez quit school at age 15, he had gone to more than 30 different schools.

By then, Cesar knew a great deal about farm work. His family did every sort of job. They planted vegetables, pruned trees, and turned grapes to make raisins. Mostly, they picked crops. They picked fruit from the trees and grapes from the vines. They dug lettuce and sugar beets out of the ground.

The life of the Chavez family was no different from the other migrant farm worker families. Children began picking crops as soon as they were able. There were laws against child labor and laws against keeping children out of school, but no one paid attention to them. The growers didn't care who harvested their crops, and migrant families needed the extra hands. It was often the only way they could earn enough money to survive.

For their work, migrants were paid 15 to 40 cents per hour. The pay depended on the season, the crop, and how many people were looking for work. There were always more workers than jobs. They could only get work through labor contractors. The contractors were paid by the growers, who owned the land. The contractors in turn hired and paid the workers, keeping much of the money for themselves. Often a contractor would call for many more workers than were needed. Then he would offer lower wages than he had promised. There was always someone willing to take the job. It was better than starving.

Because the migrant workers accepted the work so gratefully, growers assumed they were happy. But as a teenager, Cesar Chavez saw what a desperate life it was. It destroyed families, and it destroyed the human spirit. Workers would go out and get drunk on Saturday night because they could not face the truth of their lives. Their children had to work under the hot sun for 12 hours a day, even when they were sick. There was no money for a doctor anyway. In the fields, farm supervisors insulted them and bullied their children. And they took it. They had to. What else could they do? Farm labor was the only work they knew.

Years later, when the name of Cesar Chavez was praised and cursed from one end of California to the other, he would remember that feeling. He would speak of the "frustration and humiliation I felt as a boy. . . . [I] couldn't understand how the growers could abuse and exploit farm workers when there were so many of us and so few of them."

It was Cesar Chavez who would organize farm workers to stand up for their rights as Americans and as human beings. It would be his life's work to lead their struggle for dignity and self-respect.

The Chavez family had not always been migrants. Once they had owned a 160-acre farm near Yuma, Arizona. Cesar's grandfather, also named Cesar Chavez, was a poor *campesino* ("peasant farmer") in Mexico. He came north looking for a better life in the United States. The U.S. government offered free land to anyone willing to *homestead*—to live on the land five years and improve it. Many people came from Mexico to homestead in Arizona's Gila River Valley. It was a desert, but with irrigation and hard work it could be farmed. Cesar Chavez, Sr., built a large Mexican-style adobe house for his wife and 15 children. It had walls two feet thick that kept it warm in winter and cool in summer. In this house his grandson, Cesar Estrada Chavez, was born on March 31, 1927.

Like many Americans whose families came from other countries, Cesar grew up in two cultures. At home, he spoke Spanish. At school, he spoke English. On the farm, he and his brothers and sisters ate the traditional foods of Mexico. In town, they ate burgers and french fries and drank soda pop. They observed religious holidays such as Easter in the Mexican way. But they celebrated the Fourth of July and Thanksgiving as Americans.

Cesar's parents, Librado and Juana Chavez, had five children who survived. Cesar was the second oldest, after his sister Rita. Next in age was his brother Richard. Then came Eduvigis, called Vicki, and Librado, Jr., called Lennie. All of them worked on the farm. A cousin, Manuel Chavez, came to live with them as a child. He and Cesar were as close as brothers. In later years, each one often called the other "my brother," and newspapers mistakenly referred to them as brothers. Reporters liked to play up the differences between them. Here was the quick-tempered Manuel, always ready to swing a fist at anyone taking advantage of "the little guy in the fields." And there was Cesar, a different kind of fighter. His gentle face masked a stubborn strength. Cesar Chavez hated violence. There would be times when his followers grew impatient when he urged them to avoid battle with the people who oppressed them. But some of the most powerful men in California would learn just how tough he was.

His grandfather died when Cesar was still a young child. His grandmother became head of the family. But she was old and blind, and Cesar's father, Librado, ran the farm. He grew all sorts of crops—beans, melons and squash, cotton, tomatoes, and lettuce. He also raised cattle and sheep.

It was on the family farm that Cesar first got to know migrant workers. He was growing up during the Great Depression. This was a time of business failure when millions of people couldn't find work. Migrant farm workers were the poorest of the poor. They worked for pennies a day. Sometimes they worked for a bowl of food and a place to sleep.

The Chavezes were a religious family. They attended a Roman Catholic church in Yuma. Juana Chavez took seriously Jesus's words, "I was a stranger, and you welcomed me." She made a pledge never to turn away anyone who came for food. When the family lived in town, she would send her children to look for homeless people. They would invite them home for a meal. On the farm, her husband always paid his migrant help in cash each day. He built field kitchens and showers for his workers. He gave them plenty of food and a place to sleep.

The Depression touched all sorts of people. Some migrants traveled alone. Others came in family groups. There were young migrants and old. Many were Mexican Americans. Others were Chinese, Filipinos, or African Americans. There were also many *Anglos*—the Spanish word for "white Americans." Many of them had once had their own small farms in Oklahoma, Texas, or other states. Drought, dust storms, and falling farm prices had ruined them. Now they followed the crops, carrying their few belongings with them.

By 1937, the drought was over, but the Depression wasn't. There was plenty of fruit and vegetables, but not enough demand for them. Farm prices fell to their lowest point in 50 years. Each spring, then as now, farmers often had to borrow money for fertilizer, machinery, fuel, and goods for their families. They would pay it back after the fall harvest. But that year, Librado Chavez knew he would not be able to pay his debts. He could lose his farm.

The U.S. government had passed laws to help small farmers out of such trouble. It guaranteed low-interest loans. But the government could not *make* the loans. Only private banks could do that.

Librado Chavez went to a bank in Yuma. He knew his land was good land. The family had made many improvements to it. A new dam was being built nearby. It would provide more water for irrigation and raise the value of the land. Librado Chavez did not expect any problems getting a loan. But the banker in Yuma refused to grant him one.

The county seized the farm. County officials were going to sell it for the taxes and the water bill the Chavezes owed. It amounted to little more than a thousand dollars for 160 acres. A friend offered to pay their debt. The county refused to accept. It sold the land—to the banker who had refused them the loan!

"I missed that house," Cesar Chavez said years later. "When I was living there . . . it seemed like the whole world belonged to us!"

Now nothing belonged to them except the old car and what it could carry. In the fall of 1937, the Chavez family became migrant farm workers.

CHAPTER 2
Chicanos

At the age of ten, Cesar learned that few farmers treated migrants the way his parents had. Few enough treated them as well as they treated their animals.

On most jobs, the Chavezes stayed in foul labor camps. Men, women, and children lived in shacks made of cardboard, linoleum, and bits of old carpet. They slept on piles of filthy straw. Dozens of workers might share a single room. Hundreds might share a single outdoor toilet. Often there was no bath or shower. Even for such terrible living quarters, they had to pay rent. If they could not pay in advance, it was taken out of their wages.

In the fields, there were often no toilets at all. Men and women had to squat between rows of vegetables. But first they had to get permission from field supervisors. The supervisors watched over every minute of a worker's day. If a worker was moving too slowly, he or she would be sure to hear about it. Of course, there was every reason to hurry. Farm labor was piece work. Usually, the fruit pickers were paid not by the hour but by how many boxes they filled. Sometimes the growers set quotas. Workers were expected to fill so many boxes per day. Money would be subtracted from their pay for each empty box.

Workers had to pay for their tools, work gloves, and food. Often they had to buy them at company stores owned by the growers. Merchants from town charged lower prices, but they were not allowed to come onto the farms to sell to the workers. On some farms, workers could not bring drinking water into the fields. They could buy it from their supervisors at a quarter a drink. Or they could drink from the irrigation ditches.

Farm work was dangerous too. Picking some crops involved "stoop labor." Many farm workers had permanently injured backs by age 30. Then there were the trucks that carried workers to the fields. Most of them were in poor repair. Their springs and brakes were bad. There were many accidents, particularly at railroad crossings.

And there were the poisons. They were sprayed on the fields to kill insects and fungus. They also killed people, mostly children. Workers often labored in clouds of poison. It fell on their skin and into their food. It fell into the ditches they drank from. It built up in their bodies. It caused blindness, loss of muscle control, and death.

Because they needed the work, few farm workers ever complained. There was no one to complain *to*. No law protected their rights. Other workers had *unions* to bargain as a group for better pay and working conditions. This was a right American workers had fought long and hard for. Only in 1935 had the U.S. government passed a law guaranteeing workers the right to form unions. The law gave unions the right to strike. They could stop work if they felt their bosses were not bargaining fairly with them. Under the law, the bosses were not allowed to hire replacement workers, or strikebreakers.

The law did not apply to farm workers. They did not stay in one place. They moved from one job to another. How could they be organized like factory workers? Besides, the strike was too powerful a weapon for agriculture. If workers walked off their jobs at harvest time, crops would rot in the fields. Growers would be ruined.

This was how the members of Congress reasoned. The fact that many of those same members owned large farms themselves may have had something to do with their reasoning. In the past, there had been a few attempts by farm workers to form unions. They had all been beaten down by police and citizen violence.

Labor camps had been burned. Union organizers had been jailed, tortured, and killed.

In California, many of the farm workers were Mexican Americans. Added to the problems all migrants faced, they had to deal with racism too. Signs in stores and restaurants read "WHITE TRADE ONLY." Such signs also kept out African Americans and Asian Americans. But other signs made it clear what group was being singled out. They read "NO DOGS OR MEXICANS ALLOWED."

Some Anglos seemed to have a special hatred for Mexicans. California had once been a part of Mexico. The United States had taken it by force in 1846. Nearly 100 years later, Mexican culture was still strong in parts of the state. Some Anglos may have been worried that brown-skinned, Spanish-speaking people might someday take it back again if they weren't kept down. Whatever the reason, they were treated much the same way that black Americans were treated in other parts of the country. They had no rights that Anglos respected. Mexican Americans in California called themselves *Chicanos*. It was a friendly term, a short form of the Spanish word *Mexicanos*. But in the mouth of an Anglo, the word often sounded like "dirty Mexican."

Anglo growers often took this racist attitude toward the Chicanos who worked for them. They called them lazy,

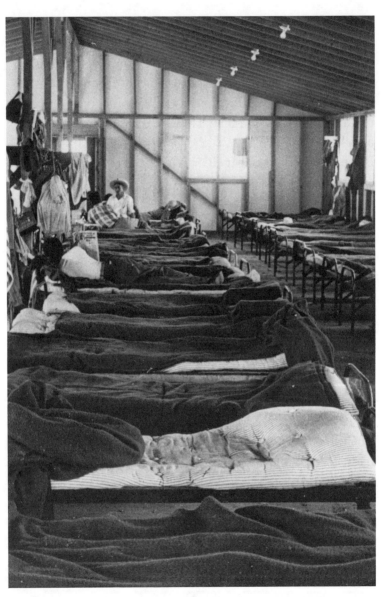

Living conditions such as these—with dozens of people sharing one room—were common for migrant farm workers in California.

and said they *deserved* low wages and filthy work camps. Why? Because they were Mexicans. Because, the growers said, they *liked* living that way.

Later, Cesar Chavez would come to see that all Mexican Americans were being kept down by the way farm workers were treated. "How could we progress as a people, even if we lived in the cities, while the farm workers—men and women of our color—were condemned to a life without pride?" he would say. "How could our people believe that their children could become lawyers and doctors and judges and business people while this shame, this injustice, was permitted to continue?"

There was also *la migra* to worry about. This was a nickname for the police who patrolled the border between the United States and Mexico. Their job was to stop people from coming into the United States illegally. The Chavezes were U.S. citizens, but *la migra* cared little for the difference between Mexicans and Mexican Americans. Whenever the family was working close to the border, Cesar's mother was terrified of being sent back to Mexico.

The Chavez family traveled the roads and scratched out a living. Cesar and his brother Richard collected foil from old cigarette packs they found by the roads. They eventually rolled it into an 18-pound ball. For this they got enough money to buy two sweatshirts and a pair of sneakers. They shared the sneakers.

Winter was the only time they stopped traveling. Librado Chavez rented a small house in San Jose, about 50 miles south of San Francisco. In 1939, he had a winter job in a factory that packed dried fruit. The workers had a union, and Cesar's father joined. That winter, the workers went out on strike for higher pay.

The strike made a deep impression on young Cesar. It was the first time he ever saw working people taking action together. The owners hired strikebreakers who were willing to work for less. *Esquiroles,* the union men bitterly called the strikebreakers—"squirrels" in Spanish. It was a name for something sneaky and cowardly. Anglo and black union men had their own name for such people—"scabs." But the strikebreakers had their own families to feed. The strike was broken, and so was the union. Librado Chavez joined other such unions that came along. They all fell apart the first time they went out on strike.

On December 7, 1941, the Japanese attacked Pearl Harbor, Hawaii. Suddenly, the United States was at war. Many campesinos left the fields to join the service or to build ships for the navy. For boys like Cesar Chavez, who were too young to go to war, it meant higher pay. For once farm labor was in short supply. Field workers could now earn as much as a dollar an hour.

The growers were not happy having to pay such wages. They got the U.S. government to work out a deal with Mexico. Mexican workers, called *braceros,* were brought in to do farm work. They were paid less than their Mexican-American cousins. But it was 15 times more than they could earn in Mexico. Their contracts were worked out between the growers and the Mexican government. As soon as the harvest was over, they were sent home. This kept them from looking for better-paying jobs. To California farm workers, the braceros were a permanent group of esquiroles.

By the time he was 16, Cesar Chavez was no longer with his family. He was traveling and working on his own. He spent most of his time near the town of Delano, California. The main crop grown there was grapes. Unlike most crops, grapes required work nine months out of the year. It was as close to a permanent job as there was in farm labor.

For Cesar, there was another reason to be near Delano. Her name was Helen Fabela. They met in the grocery store where she worked when he was 15. She invited him to go to a movie. After that, Cesar spent as much time in Delano as he could.

In 1945, Cesar turned 18. A few months later, he was drafted into the navy. By then, World War II was just about over. Cesar served on ships on weather patrol in the Pacific Ocean. He never learned to like the sea. When he was released from the navy in 1948, he returned to Delano. He and Helen were married.

A few months later, his brother Richard got married too. For a while the two couples shared a house near San Jose. Cesar and Helen began to raise a family. Their first child, a boy, was born in February 1949. Two daughters came in each of the following years.

Farm work was all the Chavez brothers knew. They joined their parents and a sister working in a strawberry field. Librado Chavez had an agreement with the grower. They were paid not by the box or the hour. Instead, they earned a share of the crop which they could then sell. Cesar realized that they were being cheated. They were working seven days a week. Their pay came out to 23 cents per hour. Cesar urged his father to quit. But Librado felt bound by the agreement he had made with the owner.

Cesar and Richard went north to work in a lumber camp. They built a cabin in the woods to live in. They both became skilled carpenters. For Richard, it became a trade. For the first time, the brothers had steady work. They could have brought their families north and made good money there. But as Richard later put it, "We'd left something behind, I guess, that we didn't want to leave.

Back in San Jose, Cesar worked picking apricots. When harvest season was over, he got a part-time job in a lumber yard. He made friends with the local parish priest. Father Donald McDonnell knew a great deal about the history of the labor movement. Cesar would accompany the priest when he said mass at nearby bracero camps. Cesar kept asking him questions about the farm labor movement. There were migrant workers in almost every state, he learned. They were exploited everywhere. There had been many attempts to organize them into unions. They all had been beaten down.

There had to be some way to help farmworkers, Cesar thought. But what could he do? He was as poor as any of them. He had never finished the seventh grade. He was living in a tough slum near an apricot orchard. The very name of the neighborhood discouraged hope. Among the Chicanos who lived there, it was called *Sal Si Puedes*—"Escape if you can." For most men, the only way out led to prison.

Then, in 1952, a stranger appeared in Sal Si Puedes who would change Cesar Chavez's life.

CHAPTER 3

Mr. Ross

At first Cesar did not want to let Fred Ross into his house. As he later told the story, "I came home from work and this gringo wanted to see me." *Gringo* means the same thing as *Anglo*, only it's a bit more insulting. The only gringos who came around Sal Si Puedes were police and university people. The police meant trouble. The university people meant nothing. They only wanted to study the way Mexicans lived. And nothing ever came of their studies.

The man first came when Cesar was at work. Helen asked him to come back later. Cesar went across the street to Richard's house and watched the gringo drive up. He'd told Helen to tell the man he was working late. But the man came back every day, and Helen got tired of lying. Finally Cesar decided to find out what he wanted.

Fred Ross worked for the Community Services Organization. The CSO was based in Chicago. It was run by a man named Saul Alinsky. It helped organize poor people for political action. Through such action, they could gain power and bring money and jobs into their communities.

The CSO wanted to organize the people who lived in Sal Si Puedes. Ross had gone to Father McDonnell for names of people he might be able to work with. Cesar Chavez's name led the list.

Chavez didn't like Ross. And it bothered Cesar that he didn't like him. Ross drove a beat-up old car and wore shabby clothes. He spoke Mexican Spanish as perfectly as any Chicano. But as far as Chavez was concerned, Ross was just another one of those university phonies. "I couldn't admit how sincere he was," Cesar later recalled.

When Ross asked him to set up a meeting, Chavez agreed. He wanted to get back at all those people who studied Mexicans as if they were animals in a zoo. He invited 20 of the roughest men in the neighborhood. He bought beer for everyone and told them his plan. They were to listen to the gringo at first and not say anything. Then, when Cesar moved his cigarette from his left hand to his right, they were to let him have it. They would curse him out, embarrass him, and make him leave. But Chavez knew he wasn't being fair. This gringo had really impressed him.

Ross spoke to the men in Spanish. Unlike the university people, he knew what their problems were. He talked about the CSO, which none of them had heard of. Then he talked about the "Bloody Christmas" case. Everyone at the meeting knew about that. In Los Angeles a few years back, drunken police officers had beaten up some Mexican prisoners. A few officers had actually gone to jail for it. Now it turned out it was lawyers from the CSO who had helped put them away.

Some of the men at the meeting still wanted to "get the gringo." They started pressing Chavez. He took them outside and told them the deal was off. "If you want to stay here and drink, okay," he said. "But if you can't shut up, get out."

It seemed so simple. Organization was power. Even the poorest community could get things done if it knew how to use the political system. The people could get a new school or a clinic built. They could get better bus service or a loan to start a new business. And Fred Ross could show them how.

That same evening, Chavez went with Ross to another meeting. Cesar was impressed by how the gringo was able to get poor, uneducated Chicanos involved in solving their own problems. No one had ever even tried to do this before. Cesar asked him about the farm workers. Could the CSO serve as a base to organize them? Ross said it could.

Cesar went to meetings with Ross almost every night. He paid attention to the way Ross did things. The man talked simply. His words drew pictures that were easy to understand. In each group, Ross picked out a person who could be a leader. Then he or she in turn could help organize other groups.

Chavez joined the CSO in organizing a voter registration drive. In two months, he registered more than 4,000 Mexican Americans who had never voted before. After the election, Saul Alinsky offered him a job on the CSO staff. It paid $35 a week. Cesar took the job. After six months in the San Jose office, he took over another CSO group Ross had started in a nearby town.

Two months later, Cesar was asked to start a group on his own. This one would be in the city of Oakland. Cesar did not like cities. He got lost in them. Going to his first meeting in Oakland, he drove back and forth in front of the house, afraid to go in. Once inside, he sat in a corner. He was too shy to identify himself as the organizer until someone asked.

His confidence grew, however. He got people to build their own organizations. Getting them started was the hardest part. Cesar taped his meetings and then listened to the tapes, trying to figure out what worked.

He was also learning to read and write—skills he had never had a chance to master in school. He read with a dictionary at his side, and with Helen nearby to help him understand the difficult ideas. He read *The Grapes of Wrath*, by John Steinbeck. It was a story about migrant farm workers during the Depression. He read books about labor unions. He read about Mexican heroes Benito Juárez and Pancho Villa. And he read about Mahatma Gandhi, the great freedom fighter of India. Cesar was struck by how Gandhi had defeated his country's enemies. He had done it through strikes, boycotts, and protest marches —the same tools labor unions used. And Gandhi had done it without violence. His people had fought violence with love. By refusing to be violent, they had shamed their enemies and won the support of the world.

Chavez thought a great deal about this. Could farm workers use Gandhi's ideas in their fight against the growers? It was natural for people to hit back when attacked. But what good would it do when the growers had the police on their side? Maybe there was another way. Would campesinos have the courage not to hit back? Would he, Cesar Chavez? This was a question he couldn't answer.

After four months, the CSO group in Oakland was working on its own. Ross asked Cesar to organize the San Joaquin Valley, the heart of California's farm country. Cesar held meetings in towns and labor camps up and down the Valley. Poverty, he knew, made farm workers afraid to take action for themselves.

He set out to win their trust. He set up a program to find lawyers for people in trouble. He helped the poorest people get welfare payments. He helped those who were citizens register to vote. He helped those who weren't citizens get the papers they needed to stay in the United States.

Other people were beginning to notice him too. Dolores Huerta worked for the CSO in Los Angeles. For years she had heard Fred Ross talk about Cesar Chavez. In 1957, she got a chance to see him in action. He was so quiet and shy that he did not seem like a leader. But she knew from his reports that he was a great organizer. "Everywhere he worked, tremendous things happened," she observed. "Those things didn't just happen by themselves."

In 1958, Chavez was named national director of the CSO. That year, he was organizing farm workers to fight the bracero program. The program was now being run by the U.S. Department of Labor. Each state was supposed to make sure that braceros were hired only when Americans were not available. The government issued work cards to the California farm workers. They could then identify themselves and be hired first. But just the opposite was happening. Growers hired braceros at lower wages while California farm workers were desperate for jobs. Chavez collected proof of hundreds of such cases. He kept careful records. In November 1959, he made his move. He had his people go into the fields and sit down opposite the braceros working there. They held a protest march to call attention to the way the government was allowing growers to break the law. At the end of the day, the workers built a fire and burned their work cards. The workers showed what they thought about how this law was enforced.

Chavez had invited the press to see the protest. Stories of crooked deals between the growers and the government made the newspapers. The growers backed down. They began to hire Chavez's people.

Throughout this time, Chavez had never lost sight of his main goal: a farm workers' union. But the CSO board would not let him start one. The organization didn't think such a union could succeed. Chavez was upset. He had been working 20 hours a day for months to organize the farm workers. He watched, frustrated, as his people were taken in by the Packinghouse union. It was part of the AFL-CIO, the nation's largest labor organization. Like all AFL-CIO unions, it was run from above. The workers did not make the decisions. Anglos in the city told them what to do. The union soon fell apart.

Every year, Chavez tried to get the CSO to let him organize a farm union. Every year they turned him down. There were too many middle-class people running the CSO, he thought. There were too few like Fred Ross. They meant well, but they weren't tuned in to the needs of the poor. To show what he thought of them, he stopped wearing a coat and tie to meetings. Instead he wore workers' clothes. He refused to shave or to cut his hair.

In March 1962, the CSO held a convention in Calexico, California, a town on the Mexican border. Chavez offered to work for a year without pay if they would let him organize a farm workers' union. Again he was turned down. "All right," he said. "I quit."

He went to a restaurant on the Mexican side of the border with Fred Ross and Dolores Huerta. He had been thinking about such a step for some time, Cesar told them. He was unhappy to have to take it. The CSO had changed his life. But his first loyalty had to be to the people he came from.

He took his wife and their large family—they now had eight children—on a vacation. They went to Carpinteria, a beach town where Cesar had once worked as a migrant. For six days, he thought and planned.

Afterward, the Chavezes went to Delano. Helen's family still lived there. Richard Chavez was there too, working as a carpenter. There would be hard times ahead, and Cesar wanted to be close to his loved ones.

CHAPTER 4
"La Causa"

Cesar had $1,200 in savings. With this money, he planned to start a national farm workers' union.

He needed people he could trust to help build it. The first ones he asked were his brother Richard and his cousin Manuel. They wanted no part of it. "Neither of us are farm workers any more!" Manuel yelled at him. He had a good job selling cars in San Diego. Richard was making good money as a carpenter. Neither of them believed that a farm union could succeed. But Cesar finally won them over.

Dolores Huerta was easier to convince. Except for Helen, she was the only one who believed in the idea from the beginning. "I would be honored to work for you," she said. Gilbert Padilla, another CSO organizer, was also among the first to join.

So too was the Reverend James Drake. He had come to Delano to work with the Migrant Ministry, a group of ministers who helped migrant workers. At first, he thought Chavez was "nuts." The man had eight kids, a broken-down old car, no money—only a dream. But he was impressed that Chavez wouldn't take money from outside interests. Jim Drake was the first Anglo to become part of the union's inner circle.

They couldn't actually call it a union. Under the law, farm workers couldn't have a union. Chavez named it the National Farm Workers Association (NFWA). But his people called it *la causa*—"the cause."

Chavez drew a map of the San Joaquin Valley. He counted 86 towns from one end to the other. In the next six months, he visited all of them. He talked to farm workers about *la causa*. He asked them to fill out cards with their name, address, and how much they thought they should be earning. He got back 80,000 cards. He was touched by how little money campesinos thought they should be paid. Most of them put down $1.15 or $1.25 an hour. Some people wrote messages such as "I hope we win." These people he visited in person.

Helen got a job picking grapes at Sierra Vista Ranch. It was owned by the Di Giorgio Corporation, one of California's biggest food producers. Sierra Vista covered 4,400 acres—nearly seven square miles. It was only one of Di Giorgio's properties, and far from the largest.

Cesar got a Sunday job digging ditches. But his money quickly ran out. He had to beg farm workers for food. It was hard on his pride, but it brought people into the union. "If people give you their food," he later commented, "they'll give you their hearts."

He used a personal approach to build the union. He sent his children to visit workers in the fields. They told the workers that if they had any problems, they should talk to Cesar Chavez. He built trust by taking a real interest in them. He put people in touch with lawyers. He sent priests to people who needed comfort. He found places to stay for migrants who were out of work. He started a credit union, a sort of private bank. Members could borrow money from it at low interest. Helen Chavez quit her job to run it.

The NFWA held its first meeting in September 1962. Two hundred and twelve members showed up. Each family paid $3.50 a month in dues. This was a lot of money for a farm worker. By paying dues, they were showing faith that something good would come of the NFWA. They were also showing that they thought of it as *their* organization.

The members were eager for action. They wanted to strike right away. But Cesar Chavez was still organizing. He said they couldn't strike and organize at the same time. Without the organization, a strike will fail. The members did not want to hear this. By July 1963, all but 12 of them had quit.

It was a bad time for the Chavez family. They had no money except what Richard was making as a carpenter. Helen's family wanted Cesar to give up the union. About this time, he was offered a good job by the U.S. government. He was asked to be a director of the Peace Corps for part of South America. The Peace Corps had been started by President Kennedy. Its volunteers helped organize people in poor countries to improve their lives. Chavez turned the job down. He wanted to organize people in California, not South America.

A private funding group offered him $50,000. He would not take it. He felt that anyone who gave him that kind of money would someday want to tell him what to do. Everyone except Dolores Huerta thought he was crazy. But they stayed with him.

Cesar kept on organizing. Farm workers up and down the Valley knew who he was. If a contractor ran off without paying them, they could talk to Cesar. If they needed medical help when their babies were being born, Cesar would know whom to call.

He started a weekly newspaper, *El Malcriado*. The name meant something like "the noisy kid," or "the brat." The paper printed names of growers who paid less than the legal minimum wage. It ran pictures of dirty, run-down labor camps. *El Malcriado* was not always a perfect newspaper. It made mistakes. But like most noisy kids, its voice got heard. Its stories led to court cases against growers who broke the law. It brought about improvements in workers' housing.

The newspaper also brought people into the union. By 1965, membership in the NFWA had grown to 1,700 families.

That May, a farm worker from a town near Delano came to see Chavez. He worked for a nursery that grew roses. Like many plants, roses are grown by grafting—joining parts of two plants together. The owners had promised the workers $9.00 per thousand for grafting roses. They were actually paying them between $6.50 and $7.00. The workers signed cards agreeing to let the NFWA bargain for them.

Chavez chose the largest nursery as the target for the NFWA's first strike. He held meetings for the workers. Strikers usually form picket lines outside their place of work. They carry signs explaining why they are striking. Picket lines keep goods from going in or out of a business. They also keep other workers away. Union members often refuse to cross other unions' picket lines. But because the NFWA was not a legal union, they could have no picket line. They would have to pledge on their honor not to go to work.

The workers voted to strike. They signed the pledge. But Cesar Chavez knew his people. Some of them would worry that the strike might fail. They would decide that no matter how miserably they were being paid, it was better than having no job at all. When the time came, they would not honor their pledge.

Early the first morning of the strike, Chavez sent people around to the workers' homes. They looked for houses with lights on. The lights told them that people were getting ready to go to work. The union people knocked on their doors. They reminded the workers of their pledge. Most of them were shamed into staying home. Not one rose worker showed up for work that day.

The owners of the nursery were furious. They refused to talk to Chavez. When Dolores Huerta came to their office to talk, they called her a communist and ordered her out. The company brought in new workers to break the strike. But rose grafting is a skill that takes time to learn. The new workers couldn't handle it. They were ruining the rose bushes.

The owners gave in. They agreed to pay the workers what they had promised. The strike was over. The NFWA had won its first victory.

Now, some of Chavez's people pressed. They felt it was time for a major strike against a big grower. However, their leader still did not think they were ready. For a big strike, they would need a much bigger union and a much stronger organization. Otherwise, the strike would easily be broken. They would have to have a strike fund to support workers while they were off the job. Chavez figured that they would not be ready until the fall of 1968.

The strike actually took place three years ahead of schedule. And it happened almost by accident.

CHAPTER 5
"¡Huelga!"

The great grape strike of 1965 began far from Delano. And at first Cesar Chavez wanted nothing to do with it.

The California grape crop is not harvested all at once. Grapes ripen first around Coachella, where the weather is hottest. By July the crop near Arvin, at the southern end of the San Joaquin Valley, is ready to be picked. The harvest then moves to the Delano area. Then it moves along the Valley, ending in early fall near Marysville. The migrant workers move with the harvest. They can always count on a vineyard needing extra hands at picking time. As for the growers, they can all get a good price, since grapes from different areas reach the market at different times. In some years, however, nature does not follow this plan.

In the Coachella Valley, a group of farm workers had formed their own union. These workers were mostly Filipinos. They were led by Larry Itliong, a Filipino

American. Like Chavez, he was careful not to call his group a union. He called it the Agricultural Workers' Organizing Committee (AWOC). But it was part of the AFL-CIO, and everyone knew it was a union.

The Coachella growers were using bracero labor. They were paying the braceros less than Chicano workers were making. The Filipinos were paid even less than the braceros. Just before the 1965 harvest season began, Itliong led the AWOC out on strike. The workers demanded to be paid the same $1.40 an hour that the Chicanos were getting.

The strike hit the growers hard. After several weeks, they gave in. They agreed to equal pay for equal work.

Later that summer, Itliong's people moved to the Delano area. There, growers were paying the same low pay that had caused the strike in Coachella. The Delano workers asked the AWOC to bargain for them. Itliong wrote to nine of the largest growers stating their demands. Five growers promised to come to a meeting to discuss them. None of them showed up. A second letter was sent out. This time there was no response. On September 8, the workers struck. For five days they stayed off the job. Then the growers brought in strikebreakers.

Itliong's people wanted to beat up the scabs. Some of them were Mexican Americans from the Delano area. The Mexican and Filipino workers did not get along well. But Itliong had worked with the CSO and knew Cesar

Chavez. He went to him and asked whether the NFWA would support his group's strike.

Chavez did not want to strike. The NFWA had less than $100 in its strike fund. He thought they just weren't ready. If they struck then and lost, they'd be broken like every other farm union.

However, some of his people had already come to him about supporting the AWOC strike. "Why are we working while our Filipino brothers are doing the right thing?" they asked him. Chavez told Itliong he'd put it to a vote of his union. He called a meeting for September 15—the eve of Mexican Independence Day.

The meeting was in Filipino Hall in Delano. This was a building used by both Filipinos and Mexicans for parties, dances, and meetings. The hall was packed with NFWA and AWOC members. Many had brought their families. A few farm supervisors mixed in with the crowd, trying not to be noticed.

Chavez spoke of Mexico's War of Independence. It had lasted ten years, and the Mexican leader had been killed, but they had won. "We Mexicans here in the United States, as well as all other farm workers, are engaged in another struggle for the freedom and dignity which poverty denies us," he said. "But it must not be a violent struggle, even if violence is used against us. Violence can only hurt us and our cause. The law is for us as well as the [growers]. Tonight we must decide if we are to join our fellow workers."

Then he called for a strike vote.

The NFWA members voted by secret ballot. The votes were counted, and Dolores Huerta announced the results. The union had voted to strike.

A cry went up: *"¡Huelga!"*—Strike! There were shouts of *"¡Viva la causa!"* and *"¡Viva la huelga!"* Long live the cause! Long live the strike! *"¡Viva Chavez!"* And so the strike was on.

It began like any other labor action. The workers stayed off their jobs. They formed picket lines at the vineyard gates to keep out strikebreakers. Right away, they discovered a problem. This was not like picketing a factory. Different fields were worked on different days. They were huge, and there were many gates. How would they know which vineyards to picket on any given day?

The union solved this problem by using scouts. Early each morning, volunteers in cars would spread out around the area. They would look for packing boxes and pickup trucks at the edge of a field. These would tell them that picking was planned there for that day. Then the volunteers would call for pickets by two-way radio. When the scabs showed up, they would find pickets marching in front of the gate. "Join us!" they would cry. "Don't scab against your brothers and sisters! Join us! ¡*Huelga!* ¡*HUEL-GA!*"

The volunteer scouts were mostly Anglo college students. Chavez knew that many of them were active in the civil rights movement and other political causes. He had visited colleges and found many Anglo students eager to help *la causa*. The radios had been borrowed from black civil rights groups. They were obtained as a result of Chavez's talent for organizing.

Early in the strike, Larry Itliong had agreed to let him speak for both unions. That way, there would be no question who was in charge. At once Chavez asked the black groups for their help. They had experience in handling picket lines. Many had worked with Martin Luther King, Jr., and other leaders who followed the teachings of Gandhi. They had the confidence and training to face angry police officers without becoming viloent. They in turn could help train the striking campesinos. Soon workers on the picket line were singing the song of the civil rights movement, "We Shall Overcome." Only they sang the words in Spanish—"Nosotros Venceremos."

Chavez organized a food program for strikers' families. He got donations of food from all over California. He saw that every family got five dollars a week in expense money. For that, he got support from other unions. Chavez still did not care for AFL-CIO methods of organizing, and they did not care for his. "You're running a civil rights movement, not a union!" one told him. But the AFL-CIO gave the farm workers $5,000 each month. The United Auto Workers and the Garment Workers' unions also sent money.

Religious organizations helped too. Most Mexicans were Catholics. Chavez had been making friends with priests for years. The Church, he knew, was one group that wouldn't want anything in return for their help. The priests in Delano would not take sides against the growers. Some were openly opposed to the strike. But other priests joined *la huelga.* Father Mark Day became a chaplain to the strikers. He dressed in workers' clothes and marched on the picket lines. Later, he wrote a book about the strike. California's Catholic bishops also took the side of the farm workers. They did not object to their priests' support of the strike.

There was help from other sources too. Doctors treated strikers and their families without charge. Some lawyers left their jobs to work for the union for next to nothing.

Lined up against the workers and their supporters were the grape growers and most of the Anglo community. They saw the strikers and the people who helped them as "troublemakers." Some saw everyone involved in the strike as "communists" who meant to take their property and destroy their way of life.

Most of the growers had Italian or Slavic names: Di Giorgio, Dispoto, Zaninovitch, Kovacevich. Their families had come to America as immigrants. All but a few had started out poor. They had arrived in the San Joaquin Valley when it was part desert, part swamp, and land was cheap. But they worked hard, and government water projects, paid for with tax money, helped them build their businesses.

All but the two biggest growers, Di Giorgio and Schenley, lived in the Valley. They were part of the community. As they saw it, the union wasn't. Most of them believed that the union's demands could ruin them. They felt that they took better care of their workers than the union could. They boasted that their workers were the best-paid farm workers in the state—their workers were happy. The average migrant family earned about $1,350 a year. The grape workers of Delano earned about $2,400. The growers felt that their workers didn't want a union and didn't need one.

Of course, $2,400 wasn't much at a time when the U.S. government considered a family "poor" if its income was under $3,000. Chavez, however, was after more than higher pay for grape workers. He saw the strike as a first step toward a union contract for all farm workers. He wanted a living wage and a health insurance plan. He wanted farm workers to have some control over their lives. As he saw it, what the growers really feared was not a union. It was power for Chicanos. Growers were used to calling Mexican Americans "boy." They were not used to bargaining with them as equals. They did not see them as human beings to be treated with respect. That was what a union was all about.

The strikers demanded a pay rate of $1.40 per hour, plus 25 cents per box picked. They also demanded that the growers observe state laws on working conditions. These included field toilets and clean drinking water. Finally, Chavez demanded that the growers recognize the union's right to bargain for all farm workers in the Delano area. Growers would have to hire workers through the union, not through labor contractors.

The growers gave in on the pay scale right away. They offered $1.40 an hour to anyone who would pick grapes. At this rate, they were able to find many people to work. Some union members quit the strike and went back to work. "Esquiroles!" the strikers yelled at them. But Chavez saw the pay raise as a victory. It showed that the growers were scared. They had backed down. "Wait for the other side to make mistakes" was a rule he had learned in the CSO. As he saw it, the growers had already made their first one. As for clean water and field toilets, most growers already provided them.

It was the last demand that no grower would accept. They would not bargain with any union. They refused even to talk with Chavez or Itliong. There was no such thing as a farm workers' union, they said. They were sure the strikers would cave in. People needed to work. All they had to do was wait.

CHAPTER 6
"Don't Buy Scab Grapes!"

The strike dragged on through the fall.

The grape growers had no trouble finding people to work. Some of the strikebreakers were local people, but most came from Mexico. The government had ended the bracero program, but growers could still use foreign workers if no Americans were available. They were called "green-carders" for the entry permits they carried. The law said they could not be used in place of striking workers, but this was not a legal strike.

The picketing continued. Now and then "scabs" would throw down their tools and join the strike. Growers tried to stop this from happening. They drowned out cries of "*¡Huelga!*" with their car radios. They moved workers to the middle of a field so that they could not see the pickets. Often things got ugly. Growers sprayed pickets with poison and manure. They beat up strikers while the police watched. Growers and farm supervisors ran down pickets with their cars. They attacked union leaders in the streets of Delano.

Chavez had made the strikers take a pledge of non-violence. They did not all keep it. Nonunion workers were threatened. Some were beaten up. Signs reading "A SCAB LIVES HERE" were put in front of their homes. Rocks were thrown through their windows. When a salesman deliberately ran over a striker with his car, a crowd surrounded him. They would have killed him, but Chavez stopped them. A few days later, a worker drove his car at three growers standing on the road.

Even with these incidents, for the most part, it was a peaceful strike. News reporters were amazed at how little violence there was. They began to ask questions about this man Cesar Chavez. This small, almost shy man was not like any other union organizer they had heard of. To his people, he was almost a saint.

"Nonviolence is not cowardice," he explained. "A nonviolent person must not be fearful. . . . He must know how to deal with people. . . . When the growers beat us, we did not fight back. Finally, they began to respect us for this. . . ."

It was clearly "Cesar's strike." Larry Itliong was happy to let him run it. Chavez was proving himself a natural leader. "When he talked to you," one follower remembered years later, "he let you know you were the whole world for him." Volunteers remarked that even when he was angry, he never abused people. When he told them they had done something wrong, "it didn't leave a scar."

By December, neither side had given in. The grapes had been harvested despite the strike. But the growers were worried. That year, 1965, the crop had *overlapped*. It had become ripe in several parts of the state at once. There had been too many grapes on the market. The price had dropped. Like small farmers (such as Cesar Chavez's father years before), the growers had money tied up in loans. Many of them could not afford another bad year.

Then Cesar Chavez made his next move. He called for a boycott of grapes. The NFWA asked Americans not to buy Delano grapes. Chavez asked other unions to honor the boycott. Any such action by a union was called a secondary boycott and was illegal. The growers kept reminding everyone that the NFWA was not even a union. Chavez wanted the growers to sign a contract with the NFWA anyway—the boycott would then end.

The boycott brought attention to Delano. The AFL-CIO was holding a convention in San Francisco. Walter Reuther, one of the nation's top labor leaders, announced that he was coming to Delano. His union, the United Auto Workers, had supported the farm workers from the beginning. In Delano, he was met by angry citizens. They carried signs that read "You Are Not Welcome

Here, Mr. Reuther," and "We Can Take Care of Our Own Problems."

"We will put the full support of organized labor behind your boycott," Reuther told NFWA members. "You are making history here, and we will march here together, we will fight here together, and we will win here together."

Chavez put together a boycott staff. He chose young workers and volunteers he had noticed on the picket line. He sent them to 13 cities. They had no money. They rode freight trains or hitched rides. Chavez figured that if they could not find ways to live, they would not be of much use in organizing a boycott. The workers begged unions for food, places to sleep, and office space. They got people to donate phones and printing services. They organized 10,000 volunteers to make calls and pass out leaflets.

That winter, "Don't buy scab grapes!" became a slogan. People saw it printed under the NFWA eagle in union halls. It appeared on lampposts, church bulletin boards, and car bumpers. In some towns, union railroad workers refused to unload trains carrying Delano grapes. In New York, the Transport Workers' Union printed a million leaflets. They handed them out on the city's buses and subways. In Los Angeles, TV stars announced their support of the boycott. In Boston, one volunteer organized a "Boston Grape Party." He bought boxes of Delano grapes.

Walter Reuther (center, holding picket sign), one of the country's most powerful labor leaders, was a strong supporter of the farm workers. Reuther came to Delano during the grape strike and joined Chavez on a picket line.

Then he led a march to Boston Harbor, where people dumped the grapes into the sea.

Americans began to pay attention. Many people hearing the farm workers' story chose to honor the boycott. In neighborhoods where union support was strong, some stores stopped selling Delano grapes and wine made from them. In other stores, shoppers had a dilemma: it was hard to tell whether a bottle of wine had been made from Delano grapes or grapes from elsewhere. It was even harder to know about table grapes—grapes for eating. There was no label telling where they came from.

Chavez had expected this problem. He aimed the boycott at the two largest growers, Schenley and Di Giorgio. They were both huge companies. Grapes were only a small part of their business. Schenley sold liquor; Di Giorgio sold canned vegetables and fruits. Both companies had brand names that people recognized. If they could be forced to sign a union contract, the smaller growers would follow.

The plan was working. The two companies were worried—but not because they were losing money. The strike and boycott hurt the farm workers far worse than it did them. The NFWA was almost broke. The strike was costing it $40,000 a month. Before, the union had always been able to scrape up a few dollars to help members pay rent or buy shoes for their children. Now there was no money for such things, yet the NFWA was spending $3,000 a month on phone calls. When Richard

Chavez used union funds to hold a party for volunteers, Cesar was furious.

Schenley and Di Giorgio were worried because it made them look bad. People saw them as heartless giants, with Chavez as a brave little knight. The U.S. Senate took notice. Senator Harrison Williams of New Jersey was about to bring a bill before Congress to make farm unions legal. To hear all sides of the issue, Williams' subcommittee on migrant labor would hold hearings in March in Sacramento, California's state capital.

Chavez announced that he would lead a 250-mile march from Delano to Sacramento after the hearings. The march would keep the country's attention on *la causa.* It would also put pressure on California's governor, Edmund G. "Pat" Brown, to do something about the strike.

The Senate hearings began in Sacramento on March 14. Reporters and TV cameras filled the hearing room. The growers presented their side first. They made the case that the strike was illegal and "probably led by communist agents." When Cesar Chavez's turn came, he spoke for the right of farm workers to have the same protection of the law as any other American workers. Because farm workers could not legally form unions, he said, no one had tried to bring the two sides together. Because legally the farm workers had no "side," no one had made any effort to settle the strike. Senator Williams' bill must be passed, he said, to prevent such a thing from happening again.

Cesar Chavez testified at the Sacramento hearings held by Senator Harrison Williams' subcommittee on migrant labor.

"I do not think we should ever hold another hearing . . . [on] the farm-labor problem," Chavez said. "The time is now past due for immediate action. . . . What we demand is very simple: we want equality. We do not want or need special treatment unless you abandon the idea that we are equal."

Two days later, the hearings moved to Delano. The star that day was subcommittee member Robert Kennedy. He was the brother of the late President John Kennedy, and the former attorney general of the United States. Now he was a U.S. senator from New York. He came from one of America's richest families, but he was clearly on the side of the farm workers.

The growers argued that the farm workers did not want or need a union. Kennedy picked apart their argument. He asked one grower, Martin Zaninovitch, why the growers did not let their workers vote on the question. Zaninovitch explained that it was because they were migrants—it was too hard to hold an election among people who moved around so much.

"We have the ability to get to the moon," Kennedy said, "so I think we can [set up a way] so people can vote. I don't think it answers the question [to] say, 'None of these people wants to join a union.' I heard very much the same thing in Mississippi—'Negroes don't want to vote.' You've got to give people [a chance]."

CHAPTER 7
"¡Viva Cesar Chavez!"

Two days later, on March 18, 1966, the march on Sacramento began.

It was a protest march, like the one Martin Luther King had led from Selma to Montgomery, Alabama, the year before. But Chavez called it a *peregrinación* ("religious journey"). He saw it as a prayer of forgiveness for the strikers' violence. The marchers would follow the banner of the Virgin of Guadalupe, a saint much loved by poor Mexicans.

Some volunteers who weren't Catholics didn't like this idea. Others saw no reason to be praying for forgiveness. They felt it was the growers who needed God's mercy, not they. But those who were closest to Chavez knew that religion and the struggle of the campesino were bound together in his heart.

As it happened, Chavez did little marching himself. He was bothered by a painful back injury and walked only a little each day. But his talent for organizing made the march possible. For 25 days, the farm workers and their supporters made their way north. Trucks carried food, portable toilets, and the marchers' belongings. Nurses took care of aching feet. Volunteers at every stop provided food. There were nightly performances by *El Teatro Campesino* ("The Farm Workers' Theater"). This was a group put together to spread the word about *la causa*. It was led by Luis Valdez, who later became a famous playwright and film director. The performances were about the strike, with actors as workers, growers, and esquiroles. They were played for laughs, and they received a lot of them.

The marchers reached Sacramento on Easter Sunday. Governor Brown ignored them. He was away with his family for the holiday. It was a disappointing end to the march. Even so, there was a sense of victory. A few days earlier, Schenley had agreed to a contract with the union!

The boycott had hurt Schenley. The company was getting letters of protest from all over the country. It was being pressured by other unions. The Teamsters' union, to which most of the country's truck drivers belonged, refused to cross NFWA picket lines. It threatened to stop deliveries to a supermarket chain that sold Schenley products. Then the company heard a rumor that the bartenders' union was going to boycott Schenley wines and liquors. It was a false rumor, but it caused the company to recognize the NFWA.

Chavez announced the terms of the agreement at a meeting in Delano. First, union members would be paid at least $1.75 an hour, at that time the legal minimum wage. Second, after a member put in a certain number of hours, he or she would earn paid holidays and vacations. Third, workers had to be hired from the union, not from labor contractors. There would be no more green-carder labor, unless a grower needed more help than the union could provide. Fourth, the company would take $3.50 dues each month out of every worker's pay and send it to the union. Lastly, the union agreed to end its boycott and picketing of Schenley.

After the longest farm strike in the country's history, the NFWA had won its first victory. It was now able to increase the pressure on its second target, the Di Giorgio Corporation.

Of all the growers, Di Giorgio was most hated by the workers. Chavez, who rarely spoke harshly of anyone, called its leaders "animals." The company president, Robert Di Giorgio, told a reporter that he was "as concerned for the welfare and dignity of our workers as anyone. . . . If a steelworker takes his pay out and drinks it up and doesn't provide for his family, then no one blames U.S. Steel. But if a farm worker does the same thing, it's the grower's fault. We can't be our brother's keeper. We can't be responsible for [how] our employees spend their money and their time."

After Schenley gave in, DiGiorgio was under pressure to agree to bargain with the union. But the company wanted nothing to do with Cesar Chavez. It invited the Teamsters to organize its workers instead.

A *teamster* originally meant someone who drove a team of horses. The Teamsters' union came to organize drivers of trucks, buses, and other motor vehicles. But cannery and packinghouse workers who handled farm products were Teamsters too. Along with the truck drivers, they were worried that a farm strike could put them out of work. The Teamsters had supported the NFWA. But when Di Giorgio offered to let it organize field workers at its Sierra Vista Ranch, the Teamsters found themselves competing with the NFWA.

On June 20, Di Giorgio offered to let the workers at Sierra Vista vote on which union would represent them. They could choose the Teamsters, the NFWA, or no union at all. Chavez agreed to the election. He assumed it would be held later that summer. But the next day, Di Giorgio announced that it would be held in three days, on June 24!

Chavez realized he had been tricked. Most of the workers then at Sierra Vista were strikebreakers. Chavez's own people were either on strike or working under union contracts for other growers. He learned that Di Giorgio had had the ballots for this election printed before Chavez had even agreed to the election!

Chavez went to court. He got the NFWA's name removed from the ballot. His people boycotted and picketed the election. The Teamsters won, as expected. But nearly half the workers at Sierra Vista honored the boycott and did not vote.

Chavez took his case to Governor Brown. The governor was in trouble. He was in a tough fight for re-election against a former movie actor, Ronald Reagan. Brown was a Democrat. A Mexican-American political group that nearly always supported Democrats was pressuring him to look into the Di Giorgio election. He named a private, respected group of experts in labor negotiations to learn the facts and decide what should be done.

The group called for a new election to be held on August 30. It ruled that anyone who had worked for Di Giorgio at least 15 days during the past year should be allowed to vote. But until the election, the NFWA had to stop picketing and boycotting the company.

The Teamsters had a bad reputation. Its leaders were often accused of being involved with organized crime. The union had been kicked out of the AFL-CIO. But it was the country's biggest union, and its most powerful. The NFWA was barely surviving. Many Di Giorgio workers favored the Teamsters. As they saw it, a large union could do more for them.

As Chavez saw it, the Teamsters were another city union that cared nothing for the farm workers except to take their dues. "We shook the tree and now they're trying to pick up the fruit," he said.

When Di Giorgio laid off 190 NFWA supporters, Chavez saw it as another trick. The laid-off workers could still vote in the election, it was true. But most likely they would not be anywhere near Delano at the time of the election. They would have to go elsewhere to find work.

It was hard fighting a company. It was hard fighting another union. To fight both of them working together was doubly tough. But if the NFWA lost this election, the union could fall apart.

It was Larry Itliong who came up with an idea. He suggested that Chavez combine the NFWA with his own AWOC—and take the union into the AFL-CIO!

There were people in both unions who were against the idea. Old-time leaders of the AWOC still refused to talk to Chavez. They thought his way of running a union was crazy. He and his top aides did not pay themselves salaries. Most of them worked for just five dollars a week. They let the members themselves run the strike.

As for the NFWA, some members worried that Cesar had "sold them out." And there was still bad feeling between Mexican-American and Filipino-American workers. Many Chicanos now talked of *la raza*—"the race," the Mexican people. Such talk troubled Chavez. He understood that it was an expression of pride, a way of telling Anglos "I am proud to be who I am." But this was a farm workers' movement, not a Mexican movement, and talk of *la raza* divided the workers. It set the poor against the poor. When the two unions voted to combine, two AWOC leaders went over to the Teamsters. They said that their union "didn't belong to the Filipinos any more."

However, most members of both unions were in favor of joining together. Between the AFL-CIO's size and strength and Cesar Chavez's personal leadership, they might just have the power to beat the Teamsters.

The new union was called the United Farm Workers Organizing Committee, or UFWOC. Chavez was elected president, Itliong vice-president. The Aztec eagle remained as the symbol of the new union.

It was a hot, ugly summer in Delano. Teamsters called Chavez a communist. The UFWOC called the Teamsters gangsters. Organizers from both unions shouted threats and insults at each other. But, except for a few fist fights, there was no violence.

The AFL-CIO helped bring to Delano migrant workers from as far away as Texas who had worked for Di Giorgio during the past year. It found them places to stay and helped feed their families to make up for their lost work.

On August 30, Di Giorgio's field workers voted to be represented by the UFWOC.

That night, the party at Filipino Hall went on almost until morning. Union members and their supporters

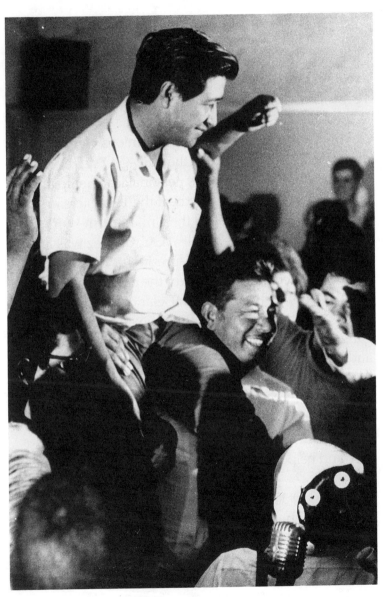

*Chavez was hoisted on the shoulders of celebrating farm workers after
the Di Giorgio field workers voted to be represented by the UFWOC.*

celebrated their victory and their leader. "*¡Viva la huelga!*" they shouted again and again. "*¡Viva la causa!*" "*¡Viva Cesar Chavez!*"

However, as sweet as their victory was, Cesar Chavez knew that the struggle was only beginning.

CHAPTER 8

The Fast

It was a victory, but it was not *the* victory.

It took seven months to work out a contract with Di Giorgio. The union won even more than it had from Schenley. Workers would get four hours' pay for any day they were called out to work and no work was available. Anyone working 1,600 hours a year for Di Giorgio got a week's paid vacation. Beginning in 1969, they would have a medical plan as well. And for the first time, farm workers would be covered by unemployment insurance.

The union celebrated its success at its new headquarters. For years, Chavez had wanted to move the union out of the collection of shacks in Delano that had been its home. In 1967, it scraped together some money to buy 40 acres of land. "Forty Acres" was a brown, muddy plot near the Delano town dump. Everyone worked in shacks and trailers while union members and volunteers planted trees and put up buildings. They built offices, meeting rooms, a health clinic, and a print shop for *El Malcriado.* Richard Chavez supervised construction. People from around the country gave food, money, and services. Volunteers did the plumbing and electrical wiring. Slowly, Forty Acres began to take shape.

Meanwhile, *la huelga* was not over. The union had won contracts with the two largest grape growers, but dozens of others had not yet signed.

Chavez went after the wine-grape growers first. Boycott organizers printed lists of wine makers who used Delano grapes. Union supporters stopped buying their products. But what finally caused the wine-grape growers to give in was an agreement between the UFWOC and the Teamsters. The two unions might have had to battle it out in every vineyard the way they had at Di Giorgio. Instead, they worked out a deal that covered all areas of farm-labor organization. The Teamsters would organize workers in canneries, warehouses, and other food-processing plants. The UFWOC would organize the field workers.

The deal was almost upset by the leaders of the AFL-CIO. Chavez was allied with the AFL-CIO now, and that group wanted no deal with the Teamsters. But some of Chavez's supporters worked things out between the different parties. In July 1967, the UFWOC and the Teamsters signed their agreement.

The growers began to cave in. The larger ones agreed to hold union elections. The smaller ones tried to hold out. But they knew they would have trouble finding workers to pick their crops when the big growers were "union." By August 1968, the UFWOC had signed contracts with 12 growers.

Now Chavez turned the boycott against table-grape growers. They still held firm against the union. They still used green-carder labor. They kept up the insults, threats, and acts of violence against pickets. At first Chavez aimed the boycott only at Giumarra, the biggest of the growers. But in 1968, he discovered that other growers across the state were secretly selling Giumarra their own labels to put on its grape boxes.

The UFWOC then targeted *all* California table-grape growers. "Don't buy scab grapes" became "Don't buy California grapes." Organizers once again traveled to cities across the country. They organized union members, students, and shoppers. They picketed supermarkets and restaurants. They spoke to officials responsible for buying food for school cafeterias. A few even went to countries in Europe to urge people not to buy California grapes.

The people listened. By then, Cesar Chavez and his workers' struggle were known around the world. Anywhere that the rights of working people were respected, the boycott found success. About 12 percent of Americans stopped eating grapes.

Chavez claimed that some of the smaller growers would have signed with the union. They were being pressured not to do so. Even some large growers thought it was stupid to keep fighting the UFWOC. Many industries, after all, had been dealing with unions for years. To many companies they were a bother, but once they accepted them, they found that they could do business with them. And whether they liked him or not, Chavez was there to stay.

However, these few growers still refused to break with the others. And most growers were still offering the same arguments: their workers were making more money than they could with a union; the union couldn't supply enough workers at harvest time and forced them to hire too many at other times; a farm can't be run like a factory. And, they maintained, Chavez and his people were a bunch of communists.

Everyone in Delano had taken sides by then. Anglos screamed curses at Chicanos in the streets. Chavez received death threats. And many farm workers were impatient with nonviolence. They felt that it was cowardly to let the growers keep taking advantage of them. Didn't strikes always involve violence? If they burned out a ranch or two, they said, the growers would pay attention.

Early in 1968, Cesar Chavez went on a money-raising trip around the country. Everywhere he went he heard talk about violence. Violence had broken out in

America's black communities the last four years, in angry protest against racism. Antiwar activists planned street violence that summer to protest the war in Vietnam. Violence was as American as apple pie, some people were saying. Violence got results.

Such talk upset Cesar Chavez. Didn't people know that violence was a sign of weakness? He believed that violence was for losers, for people who had lost all hope of winning. It was what people were left to fight with when they weren't organized. It might win a contract or two, but it would never win respect. After all this time, didn't his people know that?

On February 14, 1968, shortly after he returned home, Chavez began to fast. It was not the first time he had gone for days without eating. Fasting was a religious act for him, a form of prayer. But only a few people closest to him had known about it—his wife, his brother, and Dolores Huerta. This time he was fasting because of the anger and hatred in his own union. And so he had to tell his people.

Chavez called a special meeting on February 19. Their union, he said, had raised the hopes of poor people. They had a responsibility to those people. They couldn't let their hopes be destroyed by a few cheap victories won by violence. He asked them to look at the black civil rights movement—it was being destroyed by violence. It was black people, not whites, he said, who were being hurt by the rioting.

Then he announced his fast. He quoted what the Bible had to say about fasting. He talked about Gandhi, who had fasted to purify his heart. He told them that this was not a *hunger strike*, a political act aimed at the growers. It was an act of prayer and love for union members, taking responsibility as their leader for their actions. He would walk to Forty Acres as soon as the meeting ended. He would stay there in a shut-down gas station until he decided it was time to end the fast. Meanwhile, he would keep up his work as best he could. Then he left.

The fast nearly tore the UFWOC apart. It was not just the pro-violence groups who were angry about it. There were many who had always been uncomfortable with the religious face Chavez put on his movement. One supporter called it a "cheap publicity stunt." Another, a priest, accused Chavez of trying to set himself up as a false religious leader. Both these men quit the union.

Other people were horrified. Chavez was taking only water and vitamin pills. People who loved him feared he might die. One union man broke in with a sack of Mexican food and tried to force him to eat it. Manuel, who was guarding his cousin, had to pull the man away.

Younger men, those who had argued for violent action, went to Manuel. They swore never to use violence in union activities if he could get his cousin to give up the fast.

In fact, Cesar was checked out by a doctor before and during the fast. Except for his bad back, he was in perfect health. The fast weakened him, but he also felt that it purified him.

Chavez had asked the union to keep what he was doing quiet. But of course, the news of the fast got out. People began to gather at Forty Acres. Migrant workers brought gifts. Father Mark Day built an altar outside his door and said Mass every day for the people gathered there. Martin Luther King, who would be murdered a short time later, sent a message. He praised Chavez's courage and his work against poverty and injustice. Senator Robert Kennedy, who would be murdered in June of that year, sent his own message of concern.

The senator was in Delano on March 11, when Chavez ended his fast. The union held a huge outdoor rally at a park in town. Kennedy gave Chavez a piece of bread to mark the end of the fast.

Finally, Chavez spoke. "It is my deepest belief that only by giving our lives do we find life," he said. "I am convinced that the truest act of courage . . . is to sacrifice ourselves for others in a totally nonviolent struggle for justice. To be a man is to suffer for others. God help us be men."

The strike went on. The boycott received new support. But Chavez had shown his supporters that nonviolence was not a publicity stunt. There was no more talk of violence in support of *la causa.*

The growers also learned something from the fast. The Mexican American workers were staying peaceful only out of love and respect for their leader. Cesar Chavez

Senator Robert Kennedy, a longtime supporter of the farm workers, helped Chavez break his 25-day fast in March 1968.

was a man they could deal with. How long could he control his people?

On June 14, 1969, ten of the largest table-grape growers in California announced that they were willing to sit down and talk with Chavez and his union. Other growers gave in one by one. In July 1970, contracts were signed with 26 growers.

The grape strike and boycott that had lasted five years had been won at last.

CHAPTER 9
The Final Struggles

There would be other victories for the United Farm Workers, but none greater than the grape strike. Even before the contracts were signed, Chavez was beginning his next battle—to organize the workers in California's lettuce fields.

During the summer of 1970, the lettuce growers had agreed to let the Teamsters' union represent their field workers. Neither the growers nor the Teamsters bothered to ask the workers whether they wanted this arrangement. These agreements, Chavez told his union, "weren't contracts, they were marriage licenses." They were "sweetheart deals" that helped the growers and the Teamsters' leaders at the workers' expense. They also violated the deal worked out three years earlier between the United Farm Workers and the Teamsters.

Late in August 1970, Chavez led the lettuce workers out on strike. The action was successful at first. Nearly all the field workers honored it. The growers were losing $500,000 a day.

Then things got complicated. The workers so clearly favored the UFWOC that the Teamsters tried to back out of their contract. The growers wanted nothing to do with Chavez's union. They took the Teamsters to court to try to hold them to their contract—with workers they wanted no part of, and who wanted no part of them.

A judge ruled that the UFWOC strike was illegal. The union was ordered to end it. Chavez pulled his picket lines from the fields—and called for a boycott of lettuce not picked by the UFWOC.

Things got even more complicated. The largest of the lettuce growers, Bud Antle, had had a contract for its workers with the Teamsters since 1961. The judge ordered Chavez to stop boycotting Antle. He refused. He didn't like to challenge the contract, but the boycott could not work if its targets did not include the largest grower. For going against the court order, Chavez was thrown in jail for the first time in his life.

The jailing of Chavez was what really got the boy-cott going. The widows of Martin Luther King and Robert Kennedy announced their support. Crowds of protesters gathered outside the jail. On Christmas Eve, Chavez was released. But meanwhile, the Team-sters had announced their own boycott. Teamster drivers and packers refused to handle any crops picked by the UFWOC.

There would be other victories—but none sweeter than this announcement in 1970 that the table grape growers had reached an agreement and contract with the UFW.

What followed was a seven-year battle between the two unions for the right to organize the lettuce workers. During this time, the UFWOC's contracts with the grape growers ran out. The growers eagerly signed new deals with the Teamsters without asking the workers. The UFWOC claimed that the Teamsters' union did not represent the workers.

Teamsters from Los Angeles and other cities patrolled the fields to keep UFWOC organizers out. There were beatings and even a few shootings. UFWOC membership dropped from 55,000 in 1972 to 6,000 three years later. But the lettuce boycott continued. "This strike is not going to be lost," Chavez said in 1973. "If the growers don't sign this year, they'll sign next, and if not next year, the following. We have nothing else to do, no place else to go, and we have our patience."

In 1975, Edmund G. Brown, Jr., the son of "Pat" Brown, became governor of California. Unlike his father, "Jerry" Brown supported the right of farm labor to organize. The federal government still had no law recognizing farm unions. But Brown got such a state law passed in California. At last the United Farm Workers could call themselves a union.

Among other guarantees, the new law gave farm workers the right to choose which union should represent them. During the next two years, 312 elections were held on California's farms. The UFW won 197 of them. In March, 1977, the UFW signed another agreement with the Teamsters. It was almost exactly like the one they had signed in 1967, which the Teamsters had gone back on. But this time, it had the force of law behind it.

Since that time, the United Farm Workers' union has had its troubles. There is no question that it has helped improve the lives of farm workers. But they still remain the poorest-paid workers in the United States. Every year, machines do more and more jobs that used to be done by farm workers. The workers call them *los monstruos*—"monsters." Each year, there are fewer and fewer jobs, and workers are more willing to take whatever the growers give them. And the UFW has never been able to gain much success outside California.

Some people blamed the union's problems on Cesar Chavez himself. There were always those who felt that he was more interested in building a poor-people's movement than a labor union. One such person was Larry Itliong, who broke with Chavez in 1971. There were others who felt that Chavez, for all his talk of people building their own movement, had to control everything himself. Though he was a great organizer, he was not very good at *running* an organization. He cared nothing about note taking at meetings, record keeping, and the hundreds of other details necessary to keep a union running smoothly.

His personal magnetism began to fail him. In 1977, Chavez moved the union's headquarters from Forty Acres. He chose a new site in the mountains overlooking the San Joaquin Valley. He called it *La Paz*—"peace." But to some of his people, it seemed that he wanted them to be at war with the outside world. From time to time, he fired dozens of people at once when they questioned his ideas. Many were people who had worked for the union for years without pay. Others quit, saddened by the changes that had taken place in their leader. He accused them of being spies for the growers, communists, troublemakers, and complainers. Other practices he introduced from time to time were troubling to his supporters. And always he insisted that things be done his way.

Still, there were many people who never lost their trust in Cesar Chavez, and were willing to follow wherever he led. As one put it, "The growers don't push us around any more, they don't try to enslave us as before. That's what we're proud of."

"If the union falls apart when I am gone," Cesar Chavez said, "I will have been a miserable failure. And it would have been a terrible waste of time by a lot of people. There is no life apart from the union. It is totally fulfilling."

On April 23, 1993, Cesar Chavez died near Yuma, Arizona, not far from where he was born.

The funeral took place at Forty Acres. Cesar's brother Richard built his coffin. At the service were Helen, their 8 children, and most of their 27 grandchildren. Cesar's brothers and sisters were there, and his cousin Manuel. So too were more than 35,000 farm workers. They lined the highway out of Delano for three miles.

Among the thousands of people who turned out for the funeral of Cesar Chavez were former California Governor Jerry Brown (helping to carry casket) and the Reverend Jesse Jackson (left of Brown).

"He was a good man," said one farm worker, speaking for them all. "He was one of us."

Now that he was dead, it was left to the living to sum up Cesar Chavez's life. It was perhaps done best by Mexican-American writer Martin Espinoza: "Chavez made it clear that each of us had a right to the sort of dignity and self-respect that cannot be taken from us, because it is not given. It has always belonged to us."

Acknowledgements

The publisher and the author wish to acknowledge that the following sources were used for background information in the preparation of this biography.

Day, Mark, O.F.M., *Forty Acres: Cesar Chavez and the Farm Workers*. New York: Praeger Publishers, 1971.

Dunne, John Gregory, *Delano: The Story of the California Grape Strike*. New York: Farrar, Straus, 1967.

Matthiessen, Peter, *Sal Si Puedes*. New York: Random House, 1969.

McWilliams, Carey, *Factories in the Field: The Story of Migratory Farm Labor in California*. Santa Barbara: Peregrine Publishers, 1971.

Terzian, James, and Kathryn Cramer, *The Story of Cesar Chavez*. (juvenile). Garden City, NY: Doubleday, 1970.